How To Buy

KOREA

REAL

ESTATE

A Step-by-Step Guide to Profitable Property Investments

Youn Jae Hyeok

Youn Jae Hyeok

Copyright © 2024 by Youn Jae Hyeok

All Rights Reserved.

ISBN: 9798333458940

Imprint: Independently published

Published in the United States of America

Dedication

In the vast universe, I dedicate this book to Katarina, who showed me the beauty of gratitude.

Contents

PROLOGUE

"The best investment performance comes from finding something that others are overlooking."

-Sir John Marks Templeton

We are now in the global era. The wave of investment is flowing worldwide. In the past, foreign real estate investments were active mainly in major cities in the United States and Europe. However, with Asia's growth, this trend is shifting eastward. Starting from Hong Kong in the 1980s, real estate investment expanded to Japan, Singapore, and China.

Contrary to this movement, South Korea, which ranks 4th in Asia in terms of economic size, has not seen as much fervor in investment. This is largely due to its status as a divided country and the sensitive relationship with North Korea. Particularly, the North Korean nuclear issue has been a significant deterrent, creating negative perceptions among foreign investors.

However, South Korea's overwhelming growth, global influence, and the presence of U.S. military forces—the military of the world's strongest nation—highlight that investment in South Korea has been undervalued. Samsung, a global top company ranked 21st in market capitalization worldwide and 3rd in Asia, is headquartered in South Korea. As long as its semiconductor production facilities remain in the country, a war on the Korean Peninsula is unlikely. Semiconductors are a strategic national industry and a top priority for U.S. protection.

Moreover, as of the 2020s, South Korea is reshaping global cultural trends. Unlike the Western-dominated culture of the past, various Korean cultural contents, led by K-pop, are being imported worldwide. Music content like BTS and films like "Squid Game" and "Parasite" are sweeping the world under the banner of the Korean Wave. Soft power, such as culture, makes the younger generation aspire to visit South Korea, thereby increasing the country's investment value.

This book aims to shed light on the past and present of the Korean economy while introducing South Korean real estate to foreign investors. It also provides information on legal regulations and solutions for actual buyers, as well as promising areas for investment. Do not miss out on this new investment paradigm.

Part I

Introduction to the Korea Real Estate Market

Chapter 1: Historical Trends in Korean Economy

After World War II, the Korean Peninsula, which dreamed of reunification, was divided due to Kim Il-sung's invasion from the North. The Korean War, which began on June 25, 1950, lasted for three years, and after the war, the peninsula was divided along the 38th parallel. This line, known as the 38th Parallel, established the Democratic People's Republic of Korea (DPRK) in the north and the Republic of Korea (ROK) in the south.

North Korea, a socialist state, quickly grew based on state-led development. With the help of the Soviet Union, it rapidly advanced its heavy industries, particularly focusing on military industries, achieving significant economic development. However, by neglecting agriculture and light industries in favor of chemical industries, many North Koreans faced starvation. Consequently, North Korea has now become one of the poorest countries in the world.

South Korea, which became a democracy with the support of the United States, faced a challenging path. After the war, Korea was a small, devastated nation. It attempted to develop heavy industries like North Korea, but its neighbor, Japan, already played that role, limiting South Korea to a light industry-based economy, primarily producing textiles. However, as underdeveloped countries in Cambodia and Africa entered the light industry market with cheap labor, South Korea's competitiveness weakened.

4

To make matters worse, North Korea continued to pose threats, and U.S. President Nixon withdrew some American troops from South Korea. It was at this point that South Korea's heavy and chemical industries began to develop.

Feeling the urgency, South Korea transformed its economic structure towards heavy and chemical industries. It started producing steel and petrochemical products. After overcoming the oil crisis, a global economic boom followed. The Plaza Accord, which appreciated the Deutsche Mark and the Japanese Yen while depreciating the dollar, significantly reduced the competitiveness of Japanese products and hindered their exports. This situation allowed South Korea to gain a relative advantage. The undervaluation of the Korean Won increased the competitiveness of Korean products in the international market. Thanks to these circumstances, South Korea joined the ranks of advanced countries.

Over the next 30 years, South Korea achieved rapid growth and became known as one of the Four Asian Tigers. In a report analyzing the economic performance of major Asian countries, the World Bank referred to South Korea's economic growth as the "Miracle on the Han River," highlighting it as the best among East Asian countries.

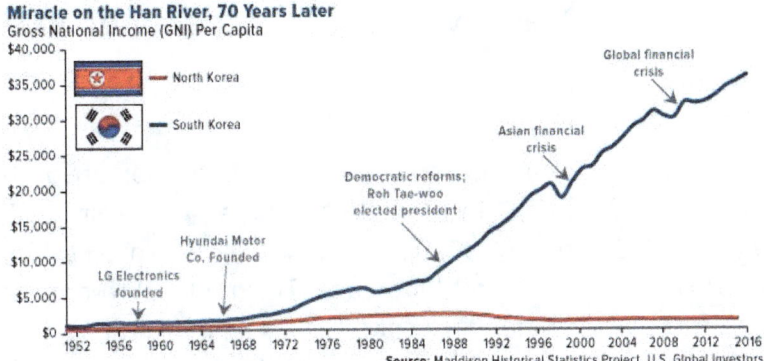

Miracle on the Han River, 70 Years Later
Gross National Income (GNI) Per Capita

<GNI Gap between South & North Korea>

Chapter 2: Overview of the Korean Economy

Now, let's look at the current economic situation of South Korea. First, the GDP. In 1960, South Korea's per capita GDP was $158.2, and by 2020, it had increased to $31,489, approximately a 200-fold increase. This ranks 25th among countries worldwide. Per capita GDP is an indicator of how affluent the citizens of a country are. In the case of South Korea, it is slightly lower than Japan but higher than Taiwan.

Next, let's examine South Korea's economy through GDP, an indicator of a country's economic growth and development level. According to statistics from the IMF and the World Bank, South Korea's GDP is approximately $2.5 trillion, ranking 12th globally. South Korea's GDP has consistently grown over the years. Notably, in 2022, South Korea surpassed Japan's GDP.

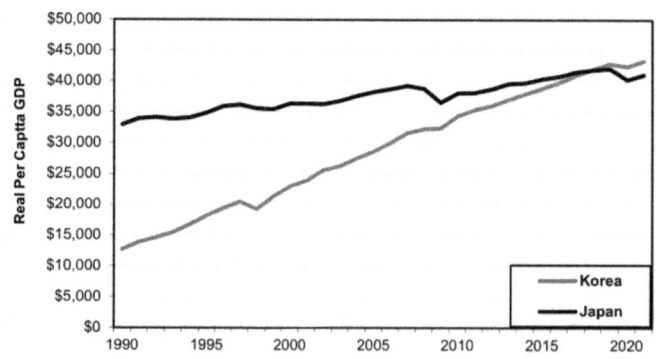

<GDP Gap between Korea and Japan>

What about South Korea's economic growth rate? According to the Bank of Korea, South Korea's economic growth rate has been increasing steadily since 1954, with only three exceptions: the 1980 oil shock, the 1998 Asian financial crisis, and the 2020 COVID-19 pandemic. This makes South Korea one of the few countries that continues to show consistent economic growth despite being an advanced country. In 2020, when the global economy was struggling due to the COVID-19 pandemic, South Korea's economic growth rate ranked 4th in the world, following China, Turkey, and Australia.

Chapter 3: Current Market Conditions

Next, let's examine the condition of the South Korean market, focusing primarily on the Consumer Price Index (CPI) and the Personal Consumption Expenditures (PCE) index. The CPI and PCE are indicators considered most important by the U.S. Federal Reserve and serve as the basis for monetary policy. The Federal Reserve's target inflation rate is 2%, and if inflation rises above this level, interest rates are increased. In other words, it is perceived as a situation of inflation.

- **Consumer Price Index (CPI)**

The Consumer Price Index (CPI) indicates the price changes of goods and services purchased by consumers. While the United States examines 8,000 items, South Korea examines 500 items to calculate the average value. However, the traditional CPI includes the prices of agricultural products and oil, which tend to fluctuate significantly due to supply chain issues. For instance, the prices of agricultural products can skyrocket due to typhoons, or oil prices can surge due to Middle Eastern conflicts, factors unrelated to a country's policies. Therefore, it is essential to look at the core Consumer Price Index.

Year	2018	2019	2020	2021	2022	2023
Core Inflation Rate (%)	1.2	0.9	0.7	1.8	4.1	4.0

South Korea's core CPI has been stable since the oil shock of 1980. Before the COVID-19 pandemic, it maintained around 1%, but it has risen to around 4% post-pandemic, which is about 1-1.5% lower than that of the United States.

- **Personal Consumption Expenditures (PCE)**

The Personal Consumption Expenditures (PCE) index is the total sum of all costs paid by the private sector for goods and services. In other words, it is the total amount spent by all 'individuals' in a country. For instance, if the PCE index increases by 0.2% in January, 0.5% in February, and 0.3% in March consecutively, it indicates that consumption is expanding and the private economy is revitalizing.

Year	2018	2019	2020	2021	2022
Per Capita Private Consumption Expenditure (Billion Won)	1,766.4	1,810.0	1,736.9	1,847.6	2,013.2
Ratio of Private Consumption Expenditure to GDP (%)	48.0	48.6	46.4	46.0	48.1

South Korea's PCE index has been steadily rising, except during the COVID-19 period. This indicates that the private economy in South Korea is continuously improving. Such growth significantly impacts the South Korean real estate market.

Part II

Why Invest in Korean Real Estate?

South Korea's stable economic growth and continuous growth potential increase the attractiveness of purchasing real estate in the country. However, the South Korean real estate market is significantly undervalued compared to the global market. Although real estate prices in South Korea nearly doubled due to interest rate cuts during the COVID-19 period, they remain relatively low on a global scale. The price per 3.3 square meters (pyeong) of an apartment in Seoul is $54,588, which is significantly lower compared to New York, Paris, Munich, and Tokyo. Particularly, it is half the price of the most expensive apartments in the world in Hong Kong.

In this chapter, we will introduce specific regions and types of real estate in South Korea that are emerging as attractive opportunities for investors. Additionally, we will explain the South Korean government's policies and incentives for foreign investors, including tax benefits and regulatory relaxations.

Chapter 4: Attractive Investment Opportunities

Introducing Specific Regions and Types of Real Estate in South Korea that are Emerging as Attractive Opportunities for Investors

■ Seoul Special Metropolitan City

First is Seoul. As the capital and largest city of South Korea, Seoul is a cultural city that harmoniously blends rivers and mountains. Serving as the capital for 1,300 years on the Korean Peninsula, Seoul is home to about ten million people, with one-third of its area covered by mountains. It has been ranked as the 7th most competitive city in the world.

Seoul is the most desired city to live in among Koreans, which means there is a high domestic demand. Therefore, investing in apartments and villas in Seoul can yield significant profits. Commercial real estate is also very popular. Seoul's three major business districts—Yeouido (YBD), Gangnam (GBD), and the Central Business District (CBD) in Seodaemun-gu—have a strong demand for office buildings and commercial spaces.

■ Incheon Metropolitan City

Next is Incheon. Incheon is a city that any foreigner visiting South Korea is likely to pass through, as it is home to Incheon International Airport. It is the closest port city to Seoul and the third-largest city in South Korea. Incheon is the only metropolitan city in South Korea with a growing population, making it a highly attractive city for real estate investment, considering the significant impact of population growth on real estate prices.

Historically, Incheon holds a critical position in Korean geography, being the landing site of General Douglas MacArthur and his troops during the Korean War. After the recapture of Incheon, UN forces advanced to Seoul in 13 days, ultimately protecting South Korea from communism.

Leveraging its geographical advantages, Incheon has developed robust manufacturing and logistics industries, with various factories centered around Incheon Port. The Incheon Free Economic Zone (IFEZ) actively attracts foreign investment with reduced taxes and regulations. South Korea has nine free economic zones for foreign investment, with Incheon being the closest to the capital.

■ Jeju Island

Jeju Island is the southernmost and largest island of South Korea. It was once an independent kingdom known as Tamna and is home to Hanlla mountain, a volcanic mountain standing 1,947 meters high. Jeju is a major tourist destination in South Korea, attracting a significant number of foreign tourists.

Jeju Island is one of the regions actively attracting foreign investment, particularly through the Real Estate Investment Immigration System, which promotes foreign investment in real estate. In 2020, the Foreign Direct Investment (FDI) in Jeju amounted to $363 million, with substantial investment in newly constructed apartments.

For foreigners wishing to reside permanently in South Korea, investing in Jeju Island is highly recommended.

Further details on other regions and specific content will be covered in Part 4.

Chapter 5: Government Policies and Incentives

Next, we will explain the South Korean government's policies and incentives for foreign investors. In 1998, South Korea changed the law regarding foreign acquisition of land from a "permission system" to a "reporting system." This change was made to attract foreign capital following the East Asian economic crisis.

• Laws Related to Foreign Real Estate Investment in South Korea

Foreigners acquiring real estate in South Korea are subject to the Foreign Land Acquisition Act, the Foreign Investment Promotion Act, and the Foreign Exchange Transactions Act. In terms of land acquisition, except for land requiring special permission, foreigners can purchase land without discrimination compared to Korean nationals. According to the Foreign Land Acquisition Act, foreigners residing in South Korea who purchase residential real estate (apartments, villas) must report the acquisition within 60 days of signing the purchase contract and then register the property ownership transfer. If the foreigner has permanent residency, they are treated the same as Korean nationals and are not subject to the Foreign Land Acquisition Act.

There is no discrimination between foreigners and Korean nationals regarding acquisition tax, property tax, and capital gains tax. The same long-term holding special deduction applied to Korean nationals is also applied to foreigners when selling the property.

Law	Foreign Land Acquisitions Act	Foreign Investment Promotion Act	Foreign Exchange Transactions Act
Subject	Foreigners (individuals, corporations, domestic corporations with over 50% foreign ownership)	Foreigners (individuals, corporations, permanent residents, international economic cooperation organizations)	Non-residents
Key Requirements	Land acquisition report	Foreign investment report	Real estate acquisition report
Reporting Agency	City hall where the land is located	Banks handling foreign exchange transactions	Banks handling foreign exchange transactions
Reporting Deadline	Within 60 days of contract signing	Before bringing in investment funds	When withdrawing funds for real estate acquisition
Governing Ministry	Ministry of Land, Infrastructure	Ministry of Trade, Industry and Energy	Ministry of Economy and Finance

• Foreign Real Estate Investment Immigration System

To stimulate the economy, South Korea introduced the Foreign Real Estate Investment Immigration System in 2010, starting with Jeju Island. This system combines real estate investment with immigration, granting residency (F-2 visa) to foreigners who invest a certain amount in designated real estate areas. After five years, permanent residency (F-5 visa) is granted.

Foreign investors eligible for the Real Estate Investment Immigration System receive various incentives in addition to permanent residency, including benefits related to education, employment, and health insurance. The designated investment areas include Jeju, Incheon (Songdo, Yeongjong, Cheongna), Busan (Haeundae, East Busan), Pyeongchang (Alpensia), and Yeosu (Geumdo), with the investment threshold set at 1 billion KRW (approximately 720,000 USD).

Category	Investment Area	Investment Amount	Period
Gangwon-do	Pyeongchang Alpensia Resort	Over 1 billion KRW	Until 2026.4.30
	Gangneung Jeongdongjin District		

Incheon	Songdo International City		
	Cheongna International City		
	Yeongjong District		
Jeju Island	Jeju Special Self-Governing Province	Over 1 billion KRW	Until 2026.4.30
Jeollanam -do	Yeosu Geumdo Marine Tourism Complex		
	Yeosu Hwayang District		
Busan City	Haeundae Tourism Resort		
	East Busan Tourism Complex		

Chapter 6: Comparison with Other Countries

What about other countries' real estate investment policies?

In recent years, many developed countries that have experienced sharp rises in real estate prices have strengthened regulations by increasing taxes on foreigners acquiring property.

Hong Kong initiated an investment immigration system in October 2003 to revive its economy. However, foreign speculative capital caused property prices in Hong Kong to quadruple over the next decade, making it difficult for local residents to buy homes. In response, the Hong Kong government increased the property acquisition tax for foreigners starting in 2010. The minimum investment amount was raised from HKD 6.5 million to HKD 10 million, and the stamp duty was increased from 8.5% to 15%. Additionally, a special transaction tax of 20% was imposed on properties sold within three years of purchase.

Singapore faced a similar situation. As low taxes attracted many investors, property prices surged. To counteract this, Singapore imposed an Additional Buyer's Stamp Duty (ABSD) of 15% on top of the existing Buyer's Stamp Duty (BSD) for foreigners. Additionally, property ownership by foreigners requires approval from the Singapore Land Authority, which is only granted if the individual can significantly contribute to the country's economy.

Vancouver, Canada also struggled with foreign real estate speculation. The province of British Columbia introduced a 15% Additional Property Transfer Tax for foreign buyers. Furthermore, due to homes being left vacant for speculative purposes, an additional 1% tax on empty homes was implemented.

Australia imposes a registration fee of AUD 10,000 for foreign buyers purchasing properties worth more than AUD 1 million. Moreover, foreigners are restricted from buying existing homes and can only purchase new properties.

Compared to these countries, South Korea's real estate market is very favorable to foreign investors. In South Korea, there is no discrimination between domestic and foreign buyers regarding property acquisition, which means there is no disadvantage when selling property later. This makes South Korea an attractive option for real estate investment.

Part Ⅲ

Type of Real Estate Investment in Korea

Chapter 7: Residential Properties

In South Korea, real estate as an investment product can be broadly categorized into four types: residential real estate, commercial real estate, industrial assets, and land. First, let's discuss residential real estate.

In South Korea, the prices of residential real estate transactions are publicly disclosed, so anyone who wishes can find out the prices at which properties have been sold. This is known as the "disclosure of actual transaction prices," and it significantly influences apartment prices because current buyers prefer to base their transactions on these disclosed prices. Due to the ease of valuation and high preference for transactions, the market operates smoothly. In particular, apartments in South Korea serve as a safe asset, much like gold, making their prices relatively stable. Additionally, about half of the South Korean population lives in these apartments.

Especially in the Seoul, Gyeonggi, and Incheon areas, where 60% of the population resides, the scarcity of land for new apartment construction has led to continuous price increases. The demand for newly built apartments is particularly high. Furthermore, with interest rate hikes leading to a significant downturn in the construction industry, the supply of new apartments has sharply decreased. Rising construction material costs have also disrupted the government's housing supply plans.

24

Therefore, apartment prices are likely to continue rising in the future.

  Next is the concept of "villa." Unlike the English meaning, in Korea, a villa (or mansion) refers to small residential buildings with four stories or less. It can be confusing, but Korean-style villas generally refer to multi-family housing units with five stories or less.

<Villa and Apartments>

Villas are generally cheaper than apartments of the same size. Because they are much more affordable than apartments in the same area, they serve as an alternative for those with limited housing budgets. Modern villas often feature robust security systems and elevators, making them a viable substitute for apartments. Additionally, older villas can provide opportunities for compensation or apartment allocation through redevelopment projects.

However, villas are often built haphazardly in alleyways, leading to frequent issues with security and access to sunlight. In response, the South Korean government has implemented policies to demolish deteriorated villas and redevelop the areas into apartment complexes, aiming to ensure citizens' housing rights. Therefore, investing in villas can potentially yield significant capital gains through future redevelopment.

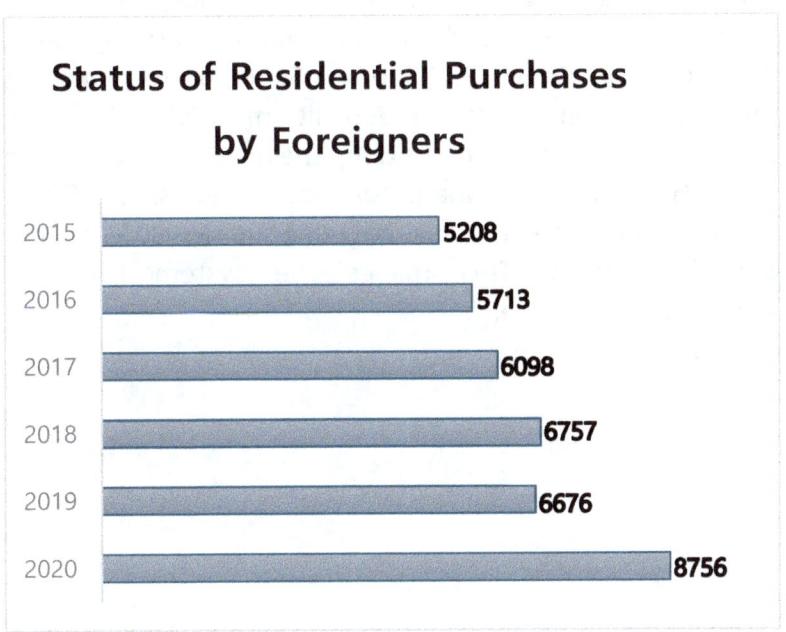

Status of Residential Purchases by Foreigners

Year	Value
2015	5208
2016	5713
2017	6098
2018	6757
2019	6676
2020	8756

※ What is Jeonse?

To understand the real estate market in South Korea, it is essential to grasp the concept of "Jeonse." Jeonse is a unique rental system that exists only in Korea. Under this system, tenants (lessees) pay a large lump-sum deposit to the landlord instead of paying monthly rent. This deposit typically amounts to 70% to 90% of the property's market value.

Thanks to this atypical Jeonse system, investors can secure substantial funds for investment. For instance, if you were to purchase a $1 million home with a Jeonse arrangement, you would only need $300,000 to $100,000 to make the purchase, depending on the deposit amount. Additionally, South Korea's public institution, the Housing Guarantee Fund (HUG), provides loans for Jeonse deposits, offering tenants low-interest loans covering up to 80% of the deposit amount. This makes the system relatively burdensome for tenants.

Chapter 8: Commercial Properties

Next, we will discuss commercial real estate, including office buildings and retail properties. Despite ongoing interest rate hikes and uncertainties in the housing market, the office market has shown relatively active movement. Notably, foreign asset management companies, often referred to as the "big players" in Korea's commercial real estate, have been significantly involved in the market.

Statistics show that in 2023, the total investment in Seoul's office market was approximately 8.2 trillion KRW (around 6 billion USD), a 40% decrease from the previous year due to interest rate impacts. Despite this reduction in investment, foreign firms remain keen on Korean offices due to their competitive edge. While global financial crises have led to increased office vacancy rates worldwide, Seoul has maintained an unusually low rate. Particularly, prime office spaces of 33,000 square meters face a supply shortage relative to demand, with companies eagerly waiting to occupy these spaces.

Seoul's vacancy rate stands at 1.5% (as of Q1 2024), which is lower compared to the previous year and lower than the natural vacancy rates of Seoul's three main office districts. The natural vacancy rate refers to the lowest vacancy rate when supply and demand are balanced.

This imbalance between supply and demand is expected to continue until 2027. The supply of prime office spaces is limited to 3 projects in 2023 and 2 projects in 2024, all of which are already leased. Hence, no new prime office supply is anticipated until 2027, indicating that low vacancy rates and high investment returns are expected in the near term. Once interest rates begin to decrease, more aggressive investors are likely to enter the office market. Additionally, foreign investors may benefit from currency exchange gains due to the strong dollar.

In the retail market, fortunes are mixed. Despite the end of the pandemic, rapid inflation and economic uncertainty have caused polarization within the retail industry. Smaller retail businesses are losing ground to the rise of online shopping.

However, larger retail companies have adapted by reducing store numbers through mergers and restructuring their business models to focus on ultra-luxury products that can only be experienced offline. Major Korean retailers are channeling their resources into high-consumption areas such as Gangnam.

Thus, profitability improvements for retail businesses are occurring in key areas of Seoul, suggesting that the retail market in these core areas will continue to rise.

Chapter 9 Industrial Properties

Next, let's discuss industrial real estate, including warehouses and factories. South Korea remains a country with a strong industrial sector. The top three export items from Korea are semiconductors, automobiles, and petrochemical products. A common characteristic of these exports is that they involve components produced across multiple factories by a single company, meaning that South Korea has a vast number of warehouses and factories. These are particularly concentrated around ports, with factories and warehouses clustering around traditional ports such as Incheon Port and Busan Port, as well as Pyeongtaek Port, which is close to China.

The monthly transaction volume for factories and warehouses in South Korea is approximately 1 trillion KRW (around 700 million USD), translating to an annual market of 15 trillion KRW (approximately 8.4 billion USD). Areas with a high concentration of small warehouses and factories, such as Hwaseong, Pyeongtaek, and Anseong in Gyeonggi Province, are popular among investors.

From 2018 to 2023, South Korea experienced an oversupply of warehouses due to a significant increase in the construction of cold storage and ambient warehouses. This oversupply led to higher vacancy rates and a notable decline in investment value. However, with the emergence of Chinese companies like Temu and AliExpress, which began aggressively leasing large warehouses in South Korea, the situation has changed. The focus on large warehouses has brought a positive shift to the warehouse market. These companies are planning to invest 200 million USD this year and 1.1 billion USD over the next three years to establish fulfillment centers (FCs), with an expectation of acquiring logistics centers near Seoul. This has attracted significant interest from investors.

Interest in industrial real estate is expected to remain strong for the time being. In particular, the prices of relatively affordable logistics centers located southeast of Seoul are continuing to rise.

Chapter 10: Land Investments

Next, let's discuss land. The land market in South Korea has distinct characteristics compared to other types of real estate. The South Korean land market operates like a luxury market. Ordinary people are not typically involved in this market; rather, it is dominated by those with investment experience or relatively wealthy individuals. They will not sell below their anticipated price, meaning that land prices do not typically decrease even during economic downturns. Investors in this blue ocean market make up less than 10% of the total investor pool.

Currently, foreign ownership of land in South Korea is very low, accounting for only 0.26% of the total land area. However, paradoxically, land is the top investment type among foreigners investing in South Korean real estate. Many foreigners and foreign companies are buying land around semiconductor manufacturing hubs like Yongin and Pyeongtaek, indicating that they see investment merit in industrial or logistics land.

Land prices in South Korea have been steadily rising, and land with large road frontage or development potential can be sold at prices significantly higher than the market value. Notably, there are no restrictions on foreign ownership of land in South Korea, making it easier to acquire compared to other countries. Additionally, there is no requirement to disclose the source of funds.

The South Korean land market is truly a niche market, known primarily to those who are in the know. Although it does not generate rental income like residential or commercial real estate, it is a lucrative investment option due to its potential for substantial capital gains.

PartIV

Understanding the Korea Real Estate Market

Chapter 11: Key Cities and Regions (Residential)

In the previous chapter, we discussed the main types of investment real estate in South Korea, including residential, commercial, and land. In this chapter, we will examine the characteristics of the real estate market by region and identify which types of real estate investments are likely to yield the best returns.

Let's start with residential real estate. Investment opportunities in residential real estate are somewhat limited to specific areas. In South Korea, the prime regions for residential investment are mainly Seoul and several areas in Gyeonggi Province, which is part of the Seoul metropolitan area.

Let's begin with Seoul.

■ SEOUL: Gangnam

Seoul is a city composed of 25 autonomous districts, which are further divided into 467 neighborhoods (dong). Just as Manhattan, Queens, and the Bronx each have distinct characteristics within New York City, each district in Seoul also has its own unique features.

Seoul's districts are categorized into different tiers, which can be visualized as a pyramid:

GangNam

Seocho
YongSan
Yeouido

Jamsil   Mokdong
Mapo   Sung-su   Jong-ro

Eunpyeng-gu   Dobong-gu   Nowon-gu
Deongbik-gu   Jungnang-gu   Gangdong-gu
Gwanak-gu   Geumcheon-gu   Guro-gu

Among Seoul's 25 districts, there are nine that offer both investment stability and profitability. At the top of this list is Gangnam, which is not only the most affluent district in Seoul but also represents the city itself.

Gangnam, famously known globally through Psy's "Gangnam Style," is located south of the Han River and is the area with the highest population density in South Korea. It boasts the most expensive real estate, the highest living standards, and extensive social infrastructure. The average price of real estate in Gangnam is around 10 million KRW per 3.3 square meters (approximately 70,000 USD), making it extremely expensive compared to cities in other countries. Despite its high prices, the value of properties in other parts of South Korea tends to follow the trends set by Gangnam. In other words, if Gangnam prices rise, so do prices in other regions. Thus, it is crucial to consider investing in apartments and villas in Gangnam due to its leading market status.

Within Gangnam, the area of Apgujeong is particularly noteworthy as a market leader. As of 2024, the most prestigious apartment in South Korea is the "Apgujeong Hyundai Apartment," with an average price of 5 billion KRW (approximately 3.6 million USD). This represents a significant increase from its 2020 price of 3 billion KRW (around 2.16 million USD). While property prices have risen in other regions as well, the increase in Gangnam's apartment prices is unparalleled. Given these factors, if you are considering investing in residential real estate in South Korea, Gangnam should be a focal point.

■ SEOUL: Yongsan

Yongsan is also a noteworthy area. The US military is stationed in the heart of Seoul, and the area where these military bases are located is Yongsan. Geographically, Yongsan is a central and pivotal location, positioned in the heart of Seoul. It is bordered by the Han River to the west and Mt.Namsan to the east, providing a unique blend of urban and natural elements within the city.

Particularly, the relocation of the Korean presidential office to Yongsan in the winter of 2022, along with the transfer of related facilities, has further enhanced its value. With Seoul's new urban plans being centered around Yongsan, there is a strong possibility that the city's core area will shift from Gangnam to Yongsan in the future.

Yongsan features a mix of apartments and single-family homes. The average price of apartments in Yongsan is around 60 million KRW per 3.3 square meters (approximately 42,000 USD), placing it among the top areas in Seoul. More astonishing are the prices for single-family homes. In Itaewon, a neighborhood within Yongsan, properties are typically priced in the range of 10 billion KRW (approximately 7.1 million USD), with prominent figures such as Samsung's Lee Jae-Yong also residing there. Given its potential for future development, Yongsan is a region that should be considered for investment.

■ SEOUL: Seongsu

Finally, let's introduce the Seongsu area in Seoul. In the past, foreign tourists visiting Korea typically explored Gangnam,

Myeongdong, and Itaewon. However, trends have shifted, and Seongsu has become a favored destination for both foreigners and Korea's younger generation. According to statistics, the number of foreign visitors to Seongsu increased from 56,000 in 2019 to 300,000 in 2024, marking a more than fivefold rise. As trend-sensitive foreigners prefer areas where they can experience the latest Korean culture over department stores and duty-free shops, Seongsu has emerged as a "hip" neighborhood.

Seongsu is characterized by its stylish buildings, flagship stores of luxury brands, and pop-up stores. Renowned brands such as Dior, Hermès, Louis Vuitton, and Chanel have opened their flagship stores in Seongsu, attracting a large influx of visitors.

The popularity of Seongsu shows no signs of waning. The company Bluehole, known for the game "Battlegrounds," has been continuously purchasing land in Seongsu, leading to a steady increase in land prices. A notable feature of Seongsu's real estate market is the high volume of corporate purchases rather than individual ones. Seongsu is the only area in South Korea where property values have more than tripled over the past three years.

Chapter 12: Key Cities and Regions (Commercial)

Having explored the investment-worthy residential areas, let's now turn our attention to commercial real estate. In Seoul, the major business districts are broadly categorized into GBD, CBD, and YBD.

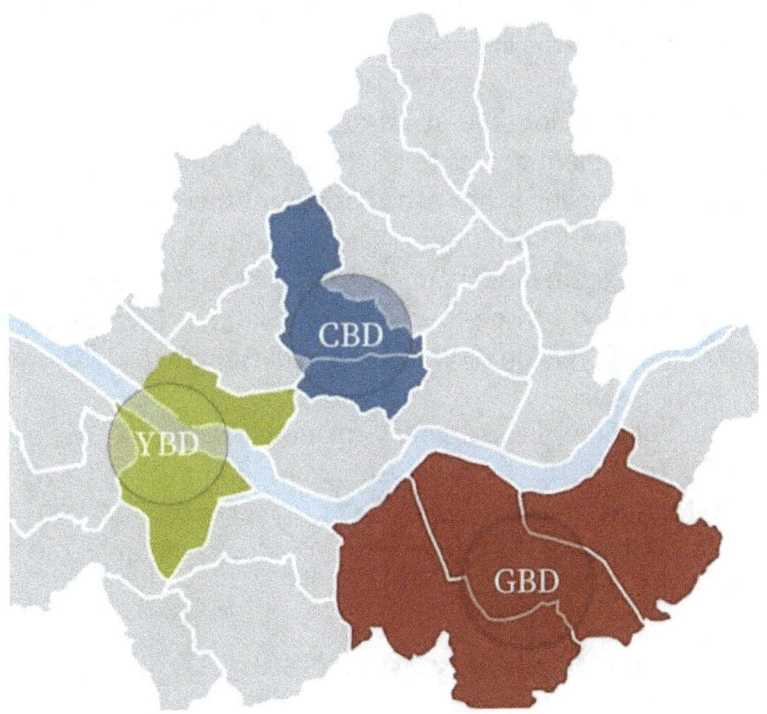

Each business district in Seoul has distinct characteristics, leading to variations in the types of businesses that lease space in these areas. Let's examine the features and rental trends of each business district.

- **Gangnam Business District (GBD)**

The Gangnam Business District (GBD) covers Gangnam-gu, along with parts of Seocho and Songpa. Centralized around Teheran-ro, it is primarily focused on IT companies. Despite higher rental rates compared to other areas, Gangnam remains a highly sought-after location for businesses ranging from startups to large corporations due to its unique status in Korea.

Gangnam, being the most developed area in Korea, provides excellent access to talent and enhances corporate image. Moreover, the area hosts numerous financial institutions and investment firms, including the Bank of Korea's Gangnam branch, making it easier to secure funding. Approximately three-fourths of large investments exceeding 100 billion KRW are made in Gangnam.

Key buildings in Gangnam include the Anam Tower, POSCO Tower, The Pinnacle Gangnam, and Parnas Tower, with Net Occupancy Costs (NOC) averaging 350,000 - 400,000 KRW per 3.3 square meters (approximately 260 - 300 USD).

- **Yeouido Business District (YBD)**

The Yeouido Business District (YBD) is centered around Yeouido Station and is known as Korea's financial hub, home to the stock exchange and various securities firms. Compared to other districts, YBD has a high supply of large office buildings. However, due to the high demand relative to supply, vacancy rates are low, with the overall office supply in Seoul being insufficient.

In 2023, YBD had a vacancy rate of 1.4%, as newly supplied offices are often pre-leased before they become available for investment, providing immediate returns.

Rental rates in YBD are lower than in GBD and CBD, and the Korean government's designation of YBD as a financial special zone with various benefits has made it a preferred location for many companies. Notable tenants include McKinsey, Samsung Securities, AIG, and Sony.

Key buildings in Yeouido include Park One, IFC, and TP Tower, with NOC ranging from 320,000 - 350,000 KRW per 3.3 square meters (approximately 240 - 260 USD).

- **Central Business District (CBD)**

The Central Business District (CBD) is centered around Gwanghwamun and Seoul City Hall, housing mainly government and public institutions, as well as foreign companies. While traditionally the political and economic center of Seoul, the CBD has been somewhat outdated. However, ongoing redevelopment and the presence of major administrative offices and embassies have kept vacancy rates low.

CBD remains a symbolic business district in Korea, attracting many traditional enterprises despite its lower modern appeal. With a workforce of 550,000, it is the largest among Seoul's business districts. Notable tenants include Microsoft and SK Group.

Key buildings in the CBD include Seoul Finance Center, Kyobo Life Building, and D-Tower, with NOC averaging 380,000 - 400,000 KRW per 3.3 square meters (approximately 280 - 300 USD).

- **Bundang Business District (BBD)**

The Bundang Business District (BBD) is located in Seongnam, Gyeonggi-do, with Pangyo Techno Valley being a representative IT industrial complex. Home to major companies like Naver and Kakao, Pangyo has become a key area connecting Seoul's three main business districts.

The successful establishment of Pangyo Techno Valley I, and the ongoing construction of Pangyo Zero City and Pangyo Techno Valley III, have solidified the area's importance.

Companies favor BBD due to its lower rental rates. Although it is very close to Gangnam, rents are about 40% cheaper, attracting numerous companies. Additionally, the concentration of ICT companies provides synergistic benefits. Hyundai Motor Group, Krafton, and Smilegate are based in this district.

Key buildings in BBD include Pangyo Innovation Valley and Mirae Asset Venture Tower, with NOC ranging from 190,000 - 220,000 KRW per 3.3 square meters (approximately 140 - 160 USD).

Summary

We have reviewed the three major business districts in Seoul and the key business district in Gyeonggi-do. All four areas feature very low vacancy rates around 1%, making them favorable for investment due to high demand. Particularly in Seoul, where there is no more space for large office buildings, the demand for offices larger than 1,000 square meters remains very high. By considering NOC when investing, you can achieve successful outcomes without failures.

District	Nearest Station	Floor Area	NOC	Rent per 3.3 ㎡
GBD	Samsung Station	848 ㎡	270 USD	90 USD
YBD	Yeouido Station	1,494 ㎡	245 USD	100 USD
CBD	Gwangwhamun Station	1,076 ㎡	250 USD	105 USD
BBD	Pangyo Station	920 ㎡	140 USD	55 USD

Chapter 13: Key Cities and Regions (Land)

Historically, foreign investors preferred land in Korea's Jeju Island or near industrial complexes with significant foreign resident populations. However, trends have shifted. Now, there is growing investment demand for land in regions where major semiconductor factories, such as those of Samsung Electronics and SK Hynix, are located. Both domestic and international investors are participating in investments in the Pyeongtaek Samsung Campus and the Yongin Hynix plant. In fact, the number of foreign investors buying land or buildings in areas like Hwaseong, Yongin, and Pyeongtaek, which actively attract foreign companies and workers, has been increasing by over 15% annually. This trend is attributed to the strong safe-haven characteristics of land prices in semiconductor cluster areas.

Let's examine the regions where semiconductor clusters are located, their characteristics, and investment points:

- **Hwaseong City**

Hwaseong has attracted significant attention from investors since the early 2010s. It is the youngest city in South Korea with an average age of 38.8 years. This is due to the presence of numerous companies including Samsung Electronics, Hyundai, and Kia. There are approximately 27,000 businesses located within Hwaseong's industrial complexes. To accommodate the growing number of companies and population, numerous land development projects are underway. The proximity to Pyeongtaek, where the semiconductor cluster is located, has contributed to a continuous increase in land prices.

- **Pyeongtaek City**

Pyeongtaek is home to Samsung's semiconductor factory and is highly favored by foreigners due to its international city status. As of 2022, it is the region in South Korea where land prices have risen the most. Pyeongtaek Port, which connects to China, hosts numerous trade-related companies and factories. This has led to a steady increase in population and ongoing new city developments. Traditionally, the southern regions of South Korea have shown higher population and economic growth rates compared to the northern part of Seoul, and Pyeongtaek stands out with exceptional economic growth rates among these southern cities.

- **Yongin City**

Yongin is an outstanding city in terms of location. It is very close to Gangnam and also near the Gyeonggi Business District (BBD), hosting IT and semiconductor-related companies. There is a lot of positive news related to the semiconductor cluster, as the South Korean government has designated Yongin as a national advanced industrial complex and is supplying a large-scale industrial park. Samsung Electronics plans to invest over 300 trillion won by 2042 to establish five advanced semiconductor manufacturing plants, which will become the world's largest and most advanced semiconductor factories upon completion. The Korean government has promised tax benefits and other support to companies entering the Yongin cluster. SK Hynix is leading the charge, starting construction of a semiconductor factory in 2025, with completion expected in 2027. It is anticipated that many partner companies will move into the area in line with this timeline.

Part V

The Investment Process

Chapter 14: Finding the Right Property

Finding the right property and conducting effective research are crucial steps in real estate investment. In Korea, most real estate listings are available online, and transaction price information for residential properties is publicly accessible. This allows investors to check market prices before making a purchase. Additionally, various proptech companies in Korea offer tools to help property seekers find properties that meet their needs.

Finding Actual Transaction Prices for Residential Properties

In Korea, the government has established the "Real Transaction Price Disclosure System" to provide transparency regarding property transactions. This system allows users to see when and at what price a property was traded. To access this information:

1. Visit rt.molit.go.kr.
2. Search for the desired property by entering its address.
3. You can view transaction prices by year.

This tool is valuable for understanding the historical transaction prices of a property, which helps in assessing its current market value.

< 'rt.molit.go.kr ' Website>

Useful Websites for Property Searches

- **Naver Real Estate**: A comprehensive platform for property listings, including detailed information on residential and commercial properties. It also provides market trends and analysis tools.
- **Zigbang**: A popular proptech company offering user-friendly tools to search for rental and sales properties, including virtual tours and price comparisons.
- **Dabang**: Another useful app for property searches that provides detailed listings, including photos and neighborhood information.
- **Kakao Real Estate**: Offers an extensive database of property listings and market information, integrated with Kakao's broader digital ecosystem.

By utilizing these tools and resources, you can make informed decisions and find properties that align with your investment goals.

Unlike residential properties, commercial real estate prices can vary widely depending on location and the condition of the building. Here are some tips and useful websites to help you find and evaluate commercial properties:

Evaluating Commercial Real Estate

1. **Location**: The location of a commercial property is crucial. Consider factors such as proximity to major roads, public transportation, and the overall economic activity in the area.
2. **Condition of the Building**: The age and condition of the building can significantly impact its value. Evaluate the maintenance history and any required renovations or repairs.
3. **Market Comparison**: Compare similar commercial properties in the area to get a sense of the market value. This involves analyzing recent transactions and understanding the trends.

Useful Websites for Finding Commercial Real Estate

- **Disco**: Disco is a useful proptech platform that provides comprehensive information on commercial real estate transactions. By entering the desired address in the search bar, you can access transaction data within a 10km radius of the specified location. This includes current market listings, allowing you to view available properties and compare them easily.

- **Naver Real Estate**: Although known for residential listings, Naver Real Estate also features commercial properties. It provides detailed information on various commercial spaces and market trends.
- **Zigbang**: Zigbang offers tools for finding commercial real estate, including virtual tours and price comparisons, which can be particularly helpful for evaluating properties remotely.

By using these platforms, you can efficiently find and assess commercial properties that meet your investment criteria.

\<Disco Website\>

Chapter 15: Working with Real Estate Agents

In Korea, real estate agents are required to hold a legal license to conduct transactions. While most agents are friendly and professional, those without experience dealing with foreign clients may be hesitant to engage in transactions with international buyers. Here are some tips for working effectively with real estate agents and understanding brokerage fees:

Working with Real Estate Agents

1. **Verify Language Skills and Experience**: If an agent lacks experience with foreign clients, they may be reluctant to handle international transactions. It is advisable to inquire whether the agent speaks English and has experience dealing with foreign buyers.
2. **Collaborate with a Consultant**: Partnering with a real estate investment consultant can be highly beneficial. These professionals have extensive experience with various agents and are well-informed about the investment area. They can help reduce risks and manage issues such as tax matters and future sales, providing a comprehensive service.

Brokerage Fees

In Korea, there are legally defined maximum brokerage fees. These fees are calculated based on the transaction amount and can be predicted in advance. The following is a table of brokerage fee rates:

Transaction Amount	Maximum Rate (Cap)
Under 50 million KRW	0.6% (up to 250,000W)
50 million ~ Under 200 million KRW	0.5%(up to 800,000W)
200 million ~ Under 900 million KRW	0.4%
900 million ~ Under 1.2 billion KRW	0.5%
1.2 billion ~ Under 1.5 billion KRW	0.6%
1.5 billion KRW and above	0.7%

Using this table, you can calculate the brokerage fee based on the property price. For example, if you purchase a property valued at 1 billion KRW, the maximum brokerage fee would be 4 million KRW. However, this is the upper limit, and fees can be negotiated below this amount.

By understanding these aspects, you can effectively collaborate with real estate agents and manage brokerage costs efficiently

Chapter 16: Negotiating and Closing Deals

In real estate transactions, where personal interactions are key, psychological skills play a crucial role. Korean people are known for their affectionate nature, meaning that emotional factors can significantly influence outcomes. Here's how to effectively negotiate and close deals:

Communicating Your Budget

Once you've conducted market research and set a budget for your property search, communicate this budget clearly to your real estate agent. It's important to specify the maximum amount you're willing to spend and avoid discussing properties that exceed this limit. Experienced agents can gauge whether a client is serious about purchasing, so sharing your budget and equity transparently can build trust and facilitate negotiations.

Understanding the Seller's Motivation

Identifying the seller's reasons for selling can give you an advantage in negotiations. For instance, if a seller needs quick cash or is facing an urgent relocation, you may be in a better position to negotiate. However, be cautious not to make overly aggressive demands that could jeopardize the deal. Striking a balance between leveraging the seller's urgency and maintaining a fair negotiation approach is key.

Securing Flexibility in Transactions

From a buyer's perspective, the timing of the final payment (balance) can be a major obstacle. Sellers typically prefer to receive the final payment quickly, but buyers may need more time due to financing or cash flow issues. Being too rigid in negotiations can risk breaking the deal. Aim for solutions that benefit both parties, such as adjusting deadlines or flexible payment terms. An open-minded approach to negotiations will help achieve a mutually beneficial outcome.

Building Rapport

Do you know about "rapport"? Rapport refers to a mutual understanding and connection between individuals. Since you're working with people, not machines or AI, building rapport with consultants and agents is essential. Trust and mutual respect can lead to the best transactions. Even though forming rapport may take time and effort, effective communication will provide valuable insights and advice, contributing to asset growth and protection.

In summary, successful real estate transactions rely on psychological insight, effective communication, and building strong relationships with all parties involved. By understanding these aspects, you can navigate negotiations and closings more effectively, ensuring a smooth and beneficial process.

Part VI

Legal and Financial Considerations

Chapter 17: Financing Options

When investing in real estate, substantial capital is often required, and financial assistance from institutions is crucial in addition to your own equity. In South Korea, real estate mortgage loans are well-established, and the maximum loan limits can be easily checked online.

Loan Amounts and Terms

1. **Commercial Real Estate and Land:**
    - **Loan-to-Value (LTV) Ratio**: For commercial properties and land, you can typically obtain a mortgage up to 60% of the purchase price or 70-80% of the appraised value. Financial institutions offer flexible terms for these assets due to their high collateral value and reliability.
    - **Commercial Property**: If the rental income from tenants is higher than market rates, you may be able to secure a larger loan amount.
    - **Land**: Generally, loans up to 80% of the appraised value are available, with principal repayment often deferred, requiring only interest payments.
2. **Residential Real Estate:**
    - **Apartments**: For properties valued under 1 billion KRW, up to 70% of the purchase

price can be financed. For properties over 1 billion KRW, the loan limit is reduced to 50%.

- o **Personal vs. Corporate Purchases**: If purchasing as an individual, the total number of properties you own will impact loan limits. For individuals with multiple properties, the loan limit decreases by 20-30%. To qualify for maximum financing, you should not own any other residential properties in Korea.

Loan Limits and Interest Rates (2024)

Property Type	Limit	Interest Rate	Notes
Apartments	70% of Purchase Price	4%-6%	Over 1 billion KRW: 50%
Office	60-70% of Appraised Value	5%-8%	Up to 60% of Purchase Price
Land	80% of Appraised Value	4.5%-6.5%	Up to 60% of Purchase Price

Chapter 18: Taxation and Legal Requirements

As Benjamin Franklin famously said, "In this world nothing can be said to be certain, except death and taxes." Understanding real estate taxes and reporting procedures is crucial for investors.

Taxes on Real Estate

In South Korea, foreign investors are subject to the same taxes as domestic investors. There are no special taxes for foreigners, ensuring equal investment conditions. The main taxes related to real estate are acquisition tax, capital gains tax, and property tax.

1. **Acquisition Tax**:
   - **Description**: Acquisition tax is levied on assets like real estate, vehicles, aircraft, ships, and memberships acquired. It must be reported and paid within 60 days of acquisition, with penalties for late reporting.
   - **Rates**:
     - **Residential Real Estate (Individuals)**: 1% - 12% (plus other taxes, totaling 1.3% - 13%)
     - **Residential Real Estate (Corporations)**: 12% (plus other taxes, totaling 13%)

- **Commercial Office**: 4% (plus other taxes, totaling 4.6%)
- **Land and Buildings**: 4% (plus other taxes, totaling 4.6%)
- **Agricultural Land**: 3% (plus other taxes, totaling 3.4%)

Type	Acquisition Tax	Other Tax	Totaling
Residential (individual)	1% ~ 12%	0.3% ~ 1%	1.3% ~ 13%
Residential(corporation)	12%	1%	13%
Commercial Office	4%	0.6%	4.6%
Land & Buildings	4%	0.6%	4.6%
Agricultural Land	3%	0.4%	3.4%

2. **Capital Gains Tax**:
   - **Description**: This tax applies to capital gains earned from asset transfers. For example, if you bought land for $100,000 and sold it for $200,000, you would pay tax on the $100,000 gain.
   - **Reporting**: Report the sale to the local tax office within 2 months of the transaction. Payment can be made via card or at a bank.
   - **Rates**:
     - **Up to 12 million KRW**: 6%
     - **12 million - 46 million KRW**: 15% (less 1.08 million KRW)
     - **46 million - 88 million KRW**: 24% (less 5.22 million KRW)

- **88 million - 150 million KRW**: 35% (less 14.9 million KRW)
- **150 million - 300 million KRW**: 38% (less 19.4 million KRW)
- **300 million - 500 million KRW**: 40% (less 25.4 million KRW)
- **500 million - 1 billion KRW**: 42% (less 35.4 million KRW)
- **Over 1 billion KRW**: 45% (less 65.4 million KRW)

Tax Base	Rate	Deduction
Up to 12 million KRW	6%	-
12 million ~ 46 million KRW	15%	1.08 M
46 million ~ 88 million KRW	24%	5.22M
88 million ~ 150 million KRW	35%	14.9M
150 million ~ 300 million KRW	38%	19.4M
300 million ~ 500 million KRW	40%	25.4M
500 million ~ 1 billion KRW	42%	35.4M
Over 1 billion KRW	45%	65.4M

3. **Property Tax**:
   - **Description**: Property tax is assessed annually based on the value of property as of June 1st. Tax bills are issued and collected by local governments.
   - **Rates**:
     - **Residential Property**:

- Up to 15 million KRW: 60,000 KRW + 0.15% of amount exceeding 60 million KRW
- Up to 30 million KRW: 195,000 KRW + 0.25% of amount exceeding 150 million KRW
- Over 30 million KRW: 570,000 KRW + 0.4% of amount exceeding 300 million KRW

- **Buildings**:
  - Factory in Designated Areas: 0.5%
  - Other Buildings: 0.25%
- **Land**:
  - Farmland/Fields/Vineyards/Forestry: 0.07%
  - Golf Courses and High-End Recreation: 4%
  - Vacant Land: 0.2% - 0.5%
  - Other Land: 0.2%

Type	Tax Base	Rate
Residential	Up to 15million KRW	60,000kwr+ 0.15%
	Up to 30million KRW	195,000krw + 0.25%
	Over 30million KRW	570,000krw + 0.4%
Buildings	Factory	0.5%
	Other	0.25%
Land	Fields	0.07%
	Golf or High Recreation	4%
	Vacant Land	0.2% ~ 0.5%
	Other	0.2%

Chapter 19: Understanding Contracts and Agreements

Once you identify a property with investment potential, the next step is to draft and finalize the contract. Real estate contracts are legally binding agreements, so it's crucial to approach them with caution.

Key Steps Before Drafting a Contract

1. **Verify the Property's Registration Certificate**
   - **Importance**: The registration certificate contains all critical information about the property, including its location, current owner, and any existing mortgages. Checking this document is an essential step.
   - **Verification Process**:
     - Ensure that the name of the owner listed on the certificate matches the name of the seller.
     - If the transaction involves a representative, verify their identity using valid identification.
     - Check for any encumbrances such as mortgages, liens, or any restrictions on the ownership rights.

2. **Review Lease and Cost Settlements**:
    - o **Tenants**: If the property has tenants, decide whether you will take over the lease or ask them to vacate. This decision must be clearly outlined in the contract to avoid potential legal disputes.
    - o **Utility Bills**: The seller is responsible for settling any outstanding utility bills (electricity, gas, water, etc.) up to the date of ownership transfer. Ensure that these bills are paid to prevent any issues with the transfer.

Contractual Procedures

1. **Deposit and Cancellation**:
    - o **Deposit**: Typically, a deposit is 10% of the total purchase price.
    - o **Cancellation Terms**:
        - If the buyer cancels the transaction, the deposit is forfeited.
        - If the seller cancels, they are required to return double the deposit to the buyer.
2. **Payment Schedule**:
    - o **Intermediate Payment**: Usually, 50% of the total amount. Once the intermediate

payment is made, the contract cannot be canceled.
- ○ **Final Payment**: After the final payment is completed, prepare the necessary documents for ownership transfer and file an application with the local registration office.
3. **Ownership Transfer**:
- ○ **Documentation**: Gather all necessary documents for the transfer and visit the relevant registration office.
- ○ **Legal Assistance**: You may seek help from a legal professional to handle this process.
- ○ **Notification for Foreigners**: According to the law, foreigners are required to report the transaction to the relevant authorities within 60 days from the contract date.

Finalizing the Contract

Once all procedures are complete and the ownership transfer is officially recorded, the real estate contract is finalized.

PartⅦ

Managing Your Investments

Chapter 20: Property Management Tips

Property management is a crucial task and neglecting it can severely limit the potential benefits of real estate investments. In other words, maintaining properties in optimal condition is key to maximizing returns.

There are fundamentally three methods of property management: self-management, outsourced management, and a hybrid approach that combines both. Self-management involves the property owner directly handling management responsibilities. However, this method is generally feasible only for small residential properties, and managing overseas properties from abroad can be exceptionally challenging. Thus, self-management is not typically recommended.

The most effective approach is outsourced management. With advancements in construction technology leading to larger and more complex buildings, a multitude of property management companies have emerged. Most real estate investors purchase properties with the goal of maximizing investment returns, which necessitates outsourcing management tasks. The advantage of outsourced management is that it allows for rational and efficient property management by leveraging the expertise of professionals. By delegating management duties, property owners can focus on their primary business or explore other investment opportunities.

However, outsourced management has its drawbacks. For example, frequent changes in management companies can lead to lapses in management quality. Additionally, if management companies focus solely on the visible aspects of the property's exterior, they might overlook issues that affect tenant comfort within the property. Therefore, it is essential to engage a reputable and comprehensive management company when opting for outsourced management.

Chapter 21: Dealing with Tenants

If you have invested in residential real estate, you will likely encounter tenants who pay monthly rent or use the "jeonse" system. In South Korea, rental agreements are typically structured for two-year terms. For jeonse agreements, which are legally protected, if a tenant wishes to extend the contract for an additional two years beyond the initial term, the rent can only be increased by up to 5%.

For jeonse arrangements, tenants often stay for four years or longer, so there are generally fewer issues to manage. Provided that there are no problems such as frozen pipes or leaks during the winter, there is little to worry about. However, with monthly rent arrangements, tenants tend to change more frequently, which may require minor repairs such as repainting, replacing flooring, or changing light fixtures. If a tenant causes damage to the property, you are entitled to recover the costs for restoration according to the law.

In cases where disputes with tenants escalate, it is advisable to have the issue handled by a consulting firm or real estate agent who assisted with the rental agreement. Resolving the matter through a third party, rather than direct confrontation, often leads to quicker and more effective solutions.

Chapter 22: Maximizing Rental Income

There are some strategies to Maximize investment return. For residential real estate, it is crucial to secure substantial "jeonse" deposits or monthly rent payments from tenants. One effective way to enhance profitability is through differentiation, and a simple method to achieve this is renovation. In Korea, renovation is often used interchangeably with the term "remodeling," referring to minor internal repairs and improvements.

Traditionally, Korea used an "ondol" heating system, which significantly influenced Korean living standards and has been adapted into modern apartment designs. This system involves installing hot water pipes under the floor to provide heating. Consequently, the core of Korean renovation often focuses on flooring. Despite the increasing use of marble flooring, Korean tenants generally prefer wooden flooring. Renovating floors with wooden materials can increase rental income and reduce vacancy rates.

Updating windows and window frames with modern building materials is another effective way to significantly lower vacancy rates. Thus, the most important elements of renovation in a residential property are flooring, windows, and clean repairs in the bathroom. Satisfying these three aspects can increase rental income by 10% to 30%.

For office spaces, slightly different strategies are employed. The key to stable office management is to encourage tenants to stay long-term. To achieve this, tenants should be given incentives to invest in the interior design of the office themselves. Since office renovations require significant investment, tenants are motivated to occupy the space for an extended period. Offering a rent-free period for a certain duration allows tenants to invest in renovations. Typically, a rent-free period of around three months is provided, during which rent, and maintenance fees are waived.

This approach serves not only to retain tenants but also to address the issue of "key money" (gwonrigum) in Korea. Key money is a payment made when acquiring an existing store or business to take over its customer base and business practices. There are various types of key money, including floor key money, business key money, and facility key money. While floor and facility key money are not recognized under international accounting standards, they are acknowledged in Korea. For instance, the key money for a prominent cosmetics store in central Seoul typically amounts to around 1 billion KRW. This high amount reflects the cost required to secure a prime location. Although key money is not legally protected, it represents an amount that tenants need to recover, creating a unique key money market. Consequently, office spaces in desirable locations almost never experience vacancies.

Offices that offer incentives such as rent-free periods for renovations are highly unlikely to face vacancies, leading to increased profitability.

Part VIII

Case Studies

Chapter 23: Successful Foreign Investment Tips

Now, let me present a successful case of real estate investment in Korea. As previously mentioned, the Korean real estate market and related regulations offer significant advantages for foreign investors. However, there is one hidden truth that has not been discussed yet: the impact of exchange rates.

The strong U.S. dollar, driven by protectionist policies in the United States, has depreciated the value of currencies other than the dollar. In practical terms, this means that if you hold dollars, you can purchase real estate in Korea at significantly reduced prices. For instance, the value of the Korean won has nearly plummeted by 30% from 2014 to 2024. This depreciation allows for discounted purchases of Korean assets when using dollars.

Let me share a case that I personally consulted on. My client, David, was the CEO of an IT company based in Silicon Valley, USA. He requested assistance in finding an office for his company's expansion into Korea. His criteria included an office space of over 600 ㎡ located in Gangnam, a prime district in Seoul. David established a corporate entity in Korea for the purpose of purchasing the office and entrusted both the establishment and the property acquisition to us.

Although establishing a foreign entity in Korea is not particularly difficult, the issue of taxes presented a challenge. Korean tax laws do not discriminate between domestic and foreign entities, but the corporate tax rate is high. To address this, I suggested relocating the office to Songdo. As mentioned earlier, the Korean government has created the Korea Free Economic Zones (KFEZ) to provide foreign-invested companies with greater economic autonomy and tax relief. Songdo, located in Incheon, is the closest economic free zone to Seoul and offers geographic advantages. Additionally, companies located in this area benefit from exemptions on customs duties, acquisition taxes, and property taxes, making it a highly attractive investment option.

David responded positively to this proposal, and ultimately, he was able to benefit from both tax incentives and favorable exchange rates when purchasing the office. Due to significant investments by global companies, office prices in Songdo have risen substantially, leading to a successful first real estate investment for David. Other CEOs, including David, have also invested in offices within the Incheon Free Economic Zone and have achieved considerable returns.

Another case involves Ms. Shulan, a private investor from Shanghai, China, who reached out via email for investment advice. In China, personal real estate ownership is restricted to usage rights only, and individuals cannot own property outright. As a result, Chinese investors are highly interested in real estate in countries where they can acquire property ownership. Korea, geographically close to China, is no exception. Many Chinese investors own numerous properties in Korea, with high demand for purchases.

Ms. Shulan was particularly interested in purchasing residential property with high investment value and potential capital gains in Seoul, with a specific request for a property with a view of the Han River. The Han River, which flows through Seoul, is traditionally associated with luxury, and homes with river views are highly sought after. Properties with such views range from 2 billion to 10 billion KRW, reflecting their high investment value and substantial price increases compared to other locations.

I recommended two undervalued apartments with Han River views, one of which doubled in value over a four-year period starting in 2018. The graph below illustrates the actual transaction prices of these properties.

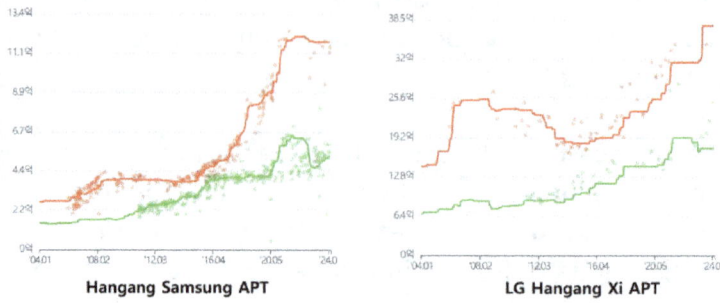

Hangang Samsung APT   LG Hangang Xi APT

This case not only demonstrates a substantial increase in property value but also highlights the crucial role of leveraging through loans. Ms. Shulan utilized a loan to finance her apartment purchase, securing 50% of the purchase price from the bank at a low interest rate. The apartment she bought was priced at 600 million KRW, and she obtained a loan for 300 million KRW, covering 50% of the purchase price. Thus, her net investment amount was 300 million KRW. When she sold the property for 1.2 billion KRW, her return on investment (ROI) was 300%.

This case serves as an excellent example of a foreign investor successfully leveraging bank financing to achieve significant returns.

Chapter 24: Lessons Learned from Failes Investments

Conversely, there are also cases of investment failure. I will present examples from clients who invested using different methods before meeting with me. These cases share a common issue: location.

As previously mentioned, the most crucial factor in real estate is location. If the location is poor, the property will not appreciate. Investments should focus on prime locations.

For instance, Mr. A purchased a 1000 m^2 plot of land in Jeju Island. In Jeju, location is extremely important due to the significant difference between properties with ocean views and those without. Additionally, the island's unique characteristics mean that additional costs are incurred for utilities like electricity and water if they are not already available. Mr. A did not verify these factors before signing the contract and ended up abandoning the purchase due to the financial burden of extending utilities and construction costs.

This case illustrates that entering into contracts without the assistance of an expert can entail significant risks.

Chapter 25: Analyzing Real Estate Deals

What Are the Key Points in Real Estate Transactions?

When you are interested in the real estate market and considering a purchase, it is crucial to seek the assistance of professional consultants and real estate agents. This is the most critical moment in the process. Typically, local real estate agents may have limited knowledge beyond their operating area.

For example, requesting a briefing on the Florida real estate market from an agent based in Los Angeles would not be professional or effective. The same principle applies in Korea. If you wish to purchase property in Seoul, you should consult with experts who have in-depth knowledge of the Seoul market. Conversely, if you are interested in acquiring land in Jeju Island, you should collaborate with specialists who are well-versed in the Jeju market.

PartIX

Resources and Tools

Chapter 26: Useful Websites and Apps

Here are some excellent websites for obtaining information on Korean real estate. First, I will introduce a site operated by the South Korean government.

This site, which is based on actual contracts for real estate transactions, is highly reliable. It provides information on residential properties such as apartments and villas, as well as land and commercial real estate transactions.

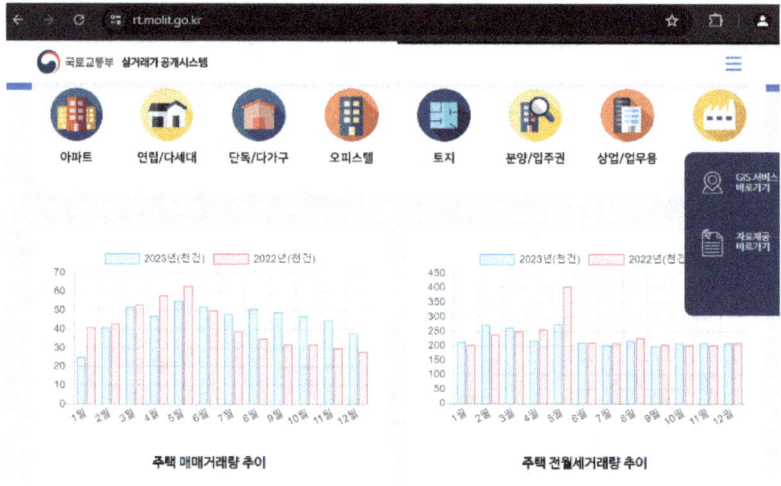

Next is 'Government 24'.

Government 24 is a website where you can access nearly all real estate-related documents online. It allows you to view materials such as cadastral maps and building registration records over the internet. Available 24/7, this site enables you to access and obtain the information you need at any time, regardless of the hour.

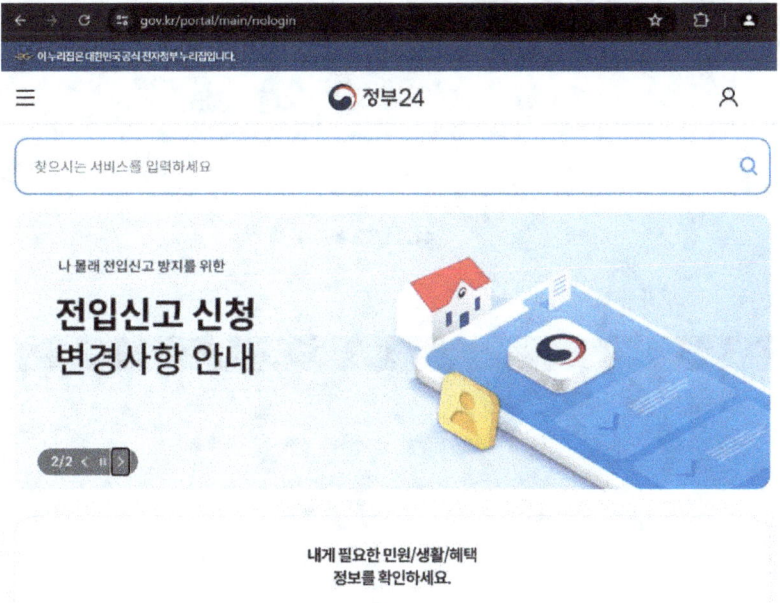

Finally, let me introduce a site that visually reconstructs real estate data based on actual transactions. This site is particularly useful as it allows for comparative analysis of recent transaction prices. As suggested by its name, the site presents valuable information mapped out for easy understanding.

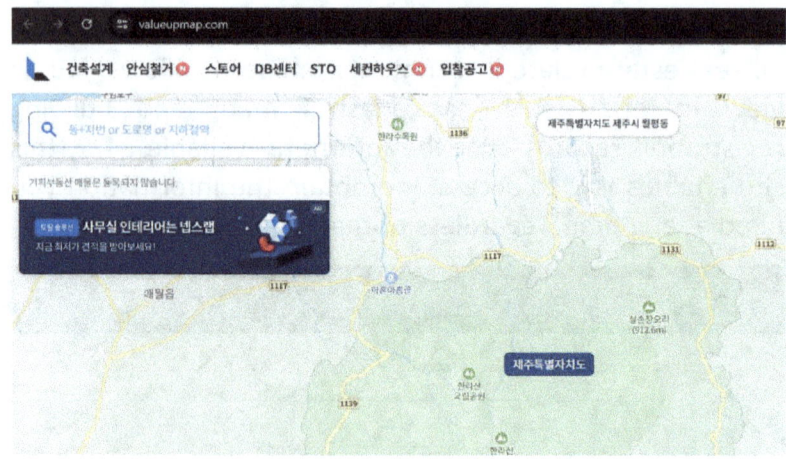

<Disco>

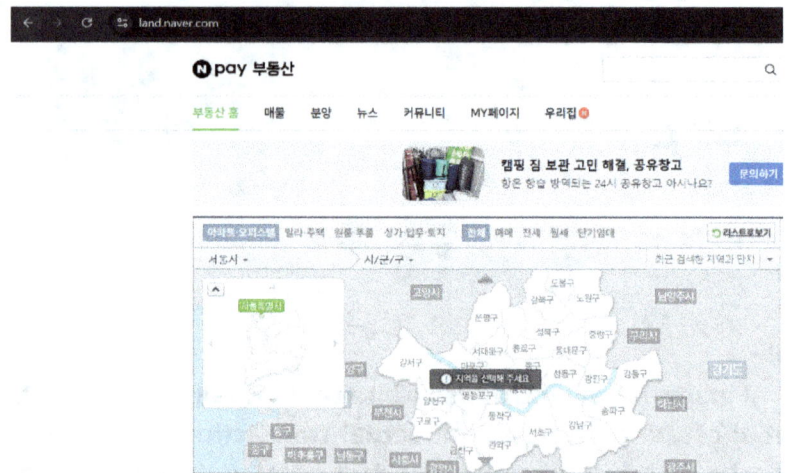

<Naver Real Estate>

Part X
Conclusion

Despite exploring various real estate investment books, I found a lack of resources specifically about investing in Korean real estate. Korea, as the world's 6th largest economy and one of the few countries to have successfully overcome IMF bailouts, shows a surprisingly low level of foreign real estate investment. Only 1% of the land in Korea is owned by foreigners, with the remaining 99% being traded among Koreans.

Historically, Korea has had a negative stance towards immigration. However, in recent years, there has been a positive shift towards immigration policies, modeled after Singapore. Korea is currently focused on growth driven by finance and investment. Although there has been an increase in foreign investors and companies in Korea since these announcements, the numbers remain relatively low. The root of this issue appears to be the lack of information.

This book aims to serve as a compass for investing in Korean real estate and, furthermore, as a fundamental guide for investment immigration in Korea. The essence of investment lies in profitability. As global economic conditions continue to become more challenging and the investment merits of advanced economies diminish, Korea presents a contrasting scenario. The Korean real estate market is a blue ocean, driven by future immigration demand and Korea's high economic growth.

If you wish to achieve substantial returns from real estate investments, I encourage you to utilize the various regions and information presented in this book. I wish you success in your investments.

About the Author

Mr. Youn is a Korean investor specializing in apartments, buildings, and land. He majored in Political Science and Business Administration in college and master's degree in real estate from graduate school. During his university years, he created an internet shopping mall through a startup program, which generated $1 million in revenue within five years before he exited the business.

Following this success, he ventured into real estate investment, buying and selling various real estate products. His investment strategy includes value investing, where he acquires assets at low prices and sells them at fair values, as well as using auctions to acquire properties. He operates three companies, and the revenue of his real estate investment firm continues to grow.

If you would like to learn more about Mr. Youn, please contact him at

realjayyoun@gmail.com.